P9-CDE-769

DISCARD

CHARGE!

Weapons
and Warfare
in Ancient Times

CHARGE!

Weapons and Warfare in Ancient Times

by Rivka Gonen

Runestone Press • Minneapolis

RUNESTONE PRESS • RᑎↃ↑ᗑ↑⦶↑

rune (r$\overline{oo}$n) *n* **1 a :** one of the earliest written alphabets used in northern Europe, dating back to A.D. 200; **b :** an alphabet character believed to have magic powers; **c :** a charm; **d :** an Old Norse or Finnish poem. **2 :** a poem or incantation of mysterious significance, often carved in stone.

Thanks to Dr. Guy Gibbon, Department of Anthropology, University of Minnesota, for his help in preparing this book.

Words in **bold** type are listed in a glossary on page 69.

Library of Congress Cataloging–in–Publication Data

Gonen, Rivka
  Charge!: weapons and warfare in ancient times/ by Rivka Gonen.
    p. cm — (Buried Worlds)
  Includes index.
  Summary: Describes the development and use of such early weapons as spears, swords, bows and arrows, and catapults as well as such means of protection as helmets, body armor, and shields.
    ISBN 0–8225–3201–8 (lib. bdg.)
    1. Weapons—]uvenile literature. 2. War—]uvenile literature. [1. Armor— History. 2. Weapons—History.] I. Title. II. Series.
  U800.G66 1993
  355.8'241—dc20
                                                          92–36772
                                                             CIP
                                                              AC

Manufactured in the United States of America
1 2 3 4 5 6 – I/JR – 98 97 96 95 94 93

CONTENTS

THE STUDY OF ANCIENT WEAPONS

For thousands of years, people have created weapons and gathered armies to fight wars. In modern times, armies use explosives and firearms to attack their enemies from long distances. Soldiers detect opposing armies with radar and use computers to aim guns and missiles. Experts push buttons to fire weapons and may not even know how much destruction is caused or how many people are killed.

This push-button warfare is very different from the warfare of ancient times, when opposing armies were often close enough to shout to one another on the battlefield. Before the development of modern technology, combatants fought hand to hand, pitting their physical strength—and the strength of their weapons—directly against one another in a fight to the death.

From the Beginning

Humans possess no natural, built-in weapons. We lack long, sharp teeth and claws, powerful hooves, and deadly horns or antlers. Although our natural weapons may not be as impressive as those of a tiger or an elephant, we are not entirely defenseless.

With an open hand, we can inflict a painful, shocking slap. With a closed fist, we can deliver a hard blow. Our nails and teeth can cause deep wounds. Even in modern times, these "biological weapons" are commonly used when humans fight, whether we are children scuffling on a playground or adults competing in a boxing match.

Our biological weapons, however, are no match for those of the large and dangerous animals that humans have hunted and killed since prehistoric times. To outfight animals—such as bears, wolves, buffalo, lions, and elephants—ancient peoples learned to use sticks, stones, and bones. They shaped

Prehistoric hunters spear a mastodon—the ancestor of the elephant. Early peoples made weapons from sticks and pointed stones.

Archaeologists—scientists who dig up and study ancient objects—unearthed these notched stone axes from a site in the South American nation of Brazil.

these objects into effective weapons and carried them at all times for protection.

The earliest people were **scavengers** (gatherers) who lived in eastern Africa about two million years ago. Their first weapons were stones, which they threw at dangerous animals and other scavengers who were some distance away. For added force, these early people probably fashioned sticks or clubs that extended the length of the human arm and increased the power of a blow. These two types of defensive movements—throwing and striking—have been used throughout human history.

For hundreds of thousands of years, humans used simple spears, axes, knives, and clubs both as tools for hunting and gathering and as dangerous weapons. Some of their weapons were designed for throwing, and some were for striking or stabbing. Tens of thousands of years ago, however, people improved their fighting ability by inventing weapons that could shoot objects farther and faster than the human arm could throw them. The first weapons of this type were the bow and arrow and the sling.

Once shooting weapons came into use, the early throwing and striking weapons became less important. Better weapons also made protection necessary. In this area, too, most animals have a natural advantage over humans.

Prehistoric peoples probably shaped stone points by striking a sharp rock with another rock or with a piece of bone or wood.

Many animals have shells or bony plates to safeguard them in case of attack. Others have thick hides or dense fur coats to shield them from the sharp teeth and claws of their enemies. When danger threatens, certain species can fly into the air, stay beneath the water, or burrow into the ground.

Natural camouflage (disguise) is also seen in the color and pattern of many animals' skins, fur, or feath-

Some animals—such as turtles (below)— withdraw into tough shells when attacked. Ancient warriors created their own protective armor from different metals. Weapon makers in China crafted this bronze helmet (left) in about 1200 B.C.

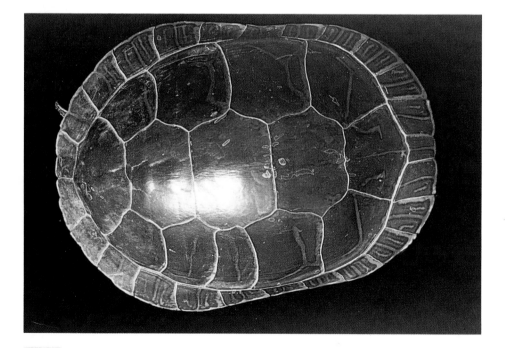

Ancient people used the first bows and arrows to hunt animals from a distance. Over time, weapon makers learned to craft bows of many different sizes with a variety of ranges.

ers. Camouflage allows animals to blend into their surroundings and become nearly invisible. Early humans had none of these natural defenses and had to rely on quickness and intelligence for protection.

As people made weapons stronger and more effective, they also learned to produce protective objects. Warriors carried shields and wore helmets and **armor** (protective body covering). To prevent attacks, people fortified their cities with thick high walls.

Only the Best

Every army wants to use the best equipment available. Because poor weapons could mean defeat and even death in battle, soldiers and military commanders were always searching for deadlier and more accurate weapons. Stronger weapons were quickly copied, however, and provided only a brief advantage. In addition, advances in offensive weapons stimulated new methods of defense.

One example of this process is the development of the bow and arrow. This weapon first appeared in about 16,000 B.C. By 5000 B.C., ancient people had begun to use the bow and arrow as a battle weapon. As warriors constructed new bows that shot farther and more powerfully, they also began to develop body armor to protect

Some metals, such as the bronze of these axheads, can be melted and reshaped. The strongest metal weapons were made from copper, bronze, and iron.

themselves from the deadly force of these weapons.

Another improvement occurred when people learned to use metals, which can be easily shaped into a variety of weapons. For most of human history, people made their weapons out of stone, bone, and wood, all of which cracked and chipped easily. None of these materials could compare with metals —such as copper and bronze—for sharpness and strength.

Metal Magic

The first metal used to make weapons was copper, which was melted down and worked into different shapes. But finished copper was soft and was easily bent or broken. Eventually, early peoples learned to make bronze—a harder and stronger metal—by adding tin to copper. In about 2500 B.C., bronze replaced copper as the most common metal for making weapons.

In about 1500 B.C., inhabitants of the Middle East learned how to form weapons from iron. They also discovered how to strengthen iron by combining it with other metals. Unlike copper and bronze weapons, which often had to be repaired, a well-made iron weapon could last a lifetime.

The development of metal weapons did not occur quickly. It took hundreds and sometimes even thousands of years to discover new ways of using and fashioning metal. Even when metalworkers had the necessary knowledge and ideas, the scarcity of metals often prevented them from improving their weapons. Many mines were jealously guarded by powerful rulers who did not want mineral ores to fall into the hands of their enemies. In addition,

A weapon smith in Central Asia crafted this iron sword in the seventh century B.C. Ancient metalworkers made the first iron weapons from meteorites—chunks of metallic matter that fall from space.

13

Archaeologists can learn about the lives of early inhabitants by studying their artwork. This wooden panel, which is inlaid with pieces of shell, shows ancient Sumerians of Mesopotamia (modern Iraq) marching into battle in 2500 B.C.

the ancient world's limited methods of transportation slowed the spread of new metals and weapons.

Some societies were reluctant to use new resources or technologies. For example, the wealthy ancient civilization of Egypt in northeastern Africa often lagged behind its neighbors in the development of new weapons. Scholars suggest that the hot, uninhabited deserts that nearly surround Egypt gave its people a sense of safety. In addition, Egyp-tians thrived on the bounty of the Nile River Valley, where dams and irrigation ditches assured a constant food supply. Made complacent by their security and wealth, Egypt's rulers resisted change.

Clues to the Past

Ancient art and literature, as well as surviving **artifacts,** provide a wealth of information about the

VULCAN, ARMORER TO THE GODS

The ancient Romans believed that gods and goddesses held power over everyday life. Roman blacksmiths and other crafts-people worshiped Vulcan, the god of fire and metalworking.

Vulcan labored in a cave under the island of Vulcania near the southern coast of Italy. Assisted by Cyclopes (one-eyed giants), Vulcan made metal objects from rivers of melted metal that flowed beneath the island.

Vulcan was most famous for arming the gods with powerful weapons. He crafted shining armor, sharp swords and spears, and great thunderbolts for Jupiter, the king of the gods. All of Vulcan's weapons were perfect, and many possessed magical qualities of strength.

The ancient Roman god Vulcan shapes a plumed helmet.

These ancient bronze dagger tips were once attached to wooden handles that decayed over time.

development of weapons. **Archaeologists**—scientists who study objects from the past—have discovered ancient weapons in tombs, in castles, and in ruined cities. Thousands of swords, spears, and axes are on display in museums around the world.

Most ancient weapons, however, did not survive intact. The wood and leather used to make weapons decayed, leaving only the metal or stone tips. In addition, because metal was difficult to obtain in ancient times, people almost never threw away broken weapons. Ancient metalworkers melted down old ax blades, spearheads, and arrow points to make new weapons.

The survival of ancient weapons also depends on the kinds of metals used to make them. Different metals decay at different rates. For example, iron rusts quickly, decomposes (breaks down), and mixes with the soil, disappearing completely within a few hundred years. Copper and bronze, on the other hand, corrode quite slowly. Weapons made from these metals may survive for thousands of years.

Some ancient weapons were placed in tombs and temples, where they were protected from the sun,

Archaeologists found two ceremonial daggers with golden sheaths (coverings) in the tomb of Tutankhamen, an ancient Egyptian pharaoh (king).

wind, and rain. Many of these were ceremonial weapons, which were often made of gold, decorated with elaborate designs, and set with precious stones. Although these weapons were not used for serious fighting, they were usually made in the shapes and styles of real weapons. By studying these ceremonial objects, archaeologists can learn about real weapons made of copper, bronze, or iron—metals that were far deadlier than anything made of gold or silver.

Ancient works of art are another important source of information about early weapons. Paintings, sculptures, seals, and other artifacts depict ancient rulers and their armies dressed for battle or actually at war. Most of these works of art show a flat view of a weapon, however, and some large and complex weapons cannot be fully understood from one angle.

Ancient writings sometimes describe how weapons were used in battle. Many ancient civilizations—including the Greeks and Romans from the Mediterranean region, the Chinese, and the Mayans from Central America—created numerous scrolls and manuscripts.

By finding and deciphering these sources of information, archaeologists have pieced together clues

The detailed painting on this container shows Etruscan soldiers in battle. The Etruscans inhabited Etruria (in modern Italy) from 650 B.C. to 450 B.C.

about ancient weapons. These experts have discovered how to operate small slings as well as mighty machines that threw huge rocks over fortress walls. These clues reveal how ancient people made, improved, and used the weapons they brought into battle.

HAND-TO-HAND COMBAT

Ancient hunters and warriors used three basic types of weapons at close range. A mace or club struck a heavy blow that stunned or wounded the victim but did not draw blood. Sabers and battle axes inflicted deep gashes. A third type of close-range weapon was meant for stabbing or piercing. Examples of piercing weapons are daggers, spears, and swords.

The Mace

The wooden club is one of the oldest of all weapons. Prehistoric people probably used many different types of clubs, but wood quickly deteriorates so few very early clubs have survived. Later societies continued to use clubs in battle and in ceremonies. Some of these clubs still exist, providing archaeologists with clues to this weapon's use in ancient times.

Early clubs were thicker and heavier on the striking end than on the grasping end. But there was a limit to how thick or how heavy a wooden club could be and still remain effective as a fighting weapon. If a fighter could not lift a club, it was useless as a weapon. As a result, ancient warriors experimented with different ways of making a club heavier but still usable. Weapon makers crafted weights that could be fastened to the end of a club. This modified weapon—called a

Ready for battle, a Mayan warrior wields a mace. The ancient Maya, who lived in Central America, also used the mace in ceremonies.

mace—could deliver a deadlier blow than a simple wooden club.

The mace consisted of two parts —a wooden handle and a doughnut-shaped head of stone or metal. Ancient peoples often carved ornate designs into these mace heads. The head was secured to the thick end of the handle so that it would not fly off in battle.

Some ancient societies considered the mace one of their most im-

Archaeologists uncovered these bronze mace heads in Israel, a country in the Middle East.

An Egyptian pharaoh prepares to strike an enemy with a mace.

portant weapons. Egyptian warriors used the mace with great skill against their enemies. Other Middle Eastern civilizations eventually abandoned the mace when it proved ineffective against soldiers wearing helmets and armor. Nevertheless, the ancient Egyptians continued to use the mace until long after other ancient peoples had abandoned it.

At one point, the Egyptians tried to improve the mace by shaping its weighted head into a disk with a sharpened edge. Although the disk gave the Egyptian mace a slight cutting action, it was not sharp enough to cut through the armor of enemy soldiers. Finally, even the conservative Egyptians abandoned the mace forever.

23

The mace has retained its ancient significance as a symbol of authority. Archaeologists have found early paintings from many civilizations, including the Mayan and the Egyptian, that show maces in the hands of kings and gods. In these paintings, the mace was a symbol of victory on the battlefield. In modern times, the mace continues to be a symbol of power and authority for monarchs and legislatures.

The Battle Ax

Unlike the mace, the battle ax—a club with an attached cutting or piercing blade—was a deadly slashing weapon that easily penetrated the helmets and armor worn by opposing armies. Over time, weapon makers developed two different types of battle axes. One had a broad, curved blade and was designed to attack the unprotected body. The other type had a long, pointed blade that could pierce enemy helmets and body armor.

One of the most difficult problems faced by the ancient weapon **smiths** (metalworkers) was **hafting** —the process of joining a weapon's metal blade to its wooden shaft. One method of hafting involved forming a long strip of metal at the end of a blade. This strip—called a **tang**—was inserted into a hole drilled in the shaft. The tang was secured to the handle with **rivets**

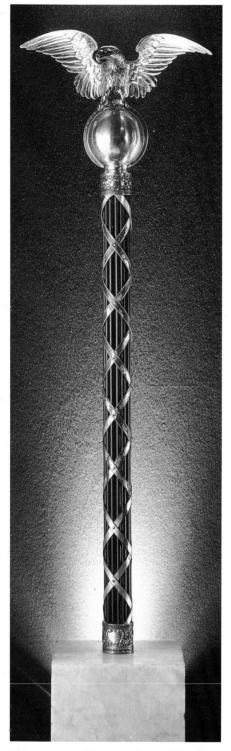

This ceremonial mace is used in the U.S. House of Representatives to indicate that the House is in session.

(metal bolts) or other binding materials. Modern kitchen knives are hafted in this way.

Smiths also used a metal tube called a socket that was attached to the end of a blade. A wooden shaft was inserted into the socket and held by rivets that passed through both the socket and the shaft. Socket hafting can be seen in modern garden shovels.

Each method of hafting had advantages. Tang hafting was quick, easy, and inexpensive. Socket haft-ing was very strong and allowed the weapon to bear tremendous stress. Because far less metal was required to make a narrow, pointed tang than a long, tubular socket, weapons made with tang hafting were lighter. As more and more armies went into battle wearing helmets and body armor, however, the use of the stronger, socket-hafted battle ax increased.

The battle ax was one of the most useful weapons of ancient times. Weapon smiths made huge

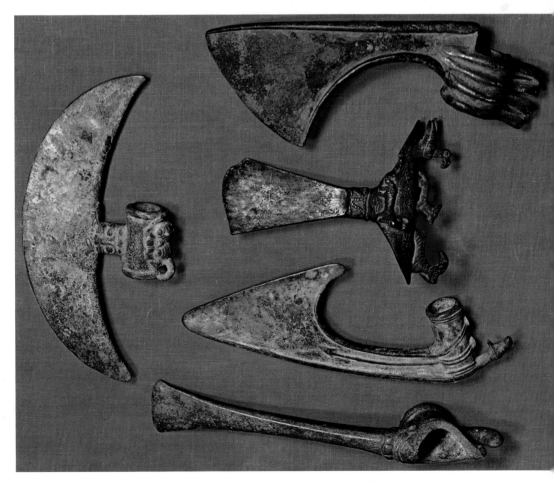

Ancient metal smiths crafted battle axes in many shapes and sizes.

axes so heavy that warriors needed both hands to lift them. They also crafted small, light axes that were designed for throwing. For example, early American Indians threw a small ax called a **tomahawk** at approaching enemies.

Like the mace, the battle ax remained important for ceremonial purposes long after it ceased to be a useful weapon in battle. The ancient Romans used the battle ax as the symbol of their rule. This symbol was revived during the 1930s when a political group arose in Europe and took its name from a Roman ceremonial battle ax called the *fasces.* The group's members called themselves fascists and used the fasces as a symbol of their power.

A mounted warrior prepares to attack an enemy with a battle ax.

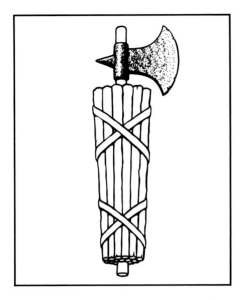

The Development of the Sword

Pictures of hand-to-hand combat in ancient times often show a fight between two brave warriors holding swords. Before 1000 B.C., however, swords were rare. The sword came into widespread use long after the mace, the battle ax, the spear, the bow and arrow, the helmet, and body armor had become standard equipment.

Although weapon makers were able to make swords by about

The fasces (above) consisted of an ax surrounded by a bundle of birch or elm rods bound together by a red strap. In ancient Rome, these bundles, which symbolized power and unity, were carried ahead of government officials. A mounted soldier (right) wields a sword of iron, the strongest metal of ancient times.

2500 B.C., early versions were not effective. Before 1000 B.C., the metals used by weapon makers were too soft and too weak for making swords. A long, thin blade of even the hardest copper or bronze could not withstand the constant clash of hand-to-hand fighting. This problem limited the length and width of the weapons artisans could make.

Early smiths also did not know how to effectively shape metal into a single long object. Most ancient weapons consisted of a long shaft to which a fairly small blade was attached. A sword is nearly all blade. Only the **hilt** (a short handle) is made of wood or bone.

The immediate ancestor of the modern sword was the bronze dagger, which was modeled after pre-

Ancient metal smiths in China made this bronze hilt to hold a hafted weapon. The holes in the side of the hilt show where a metal blade was riveted in place.

Archaeologists in Egypt discovered this well-preserved dagger and its wooden handle intact.

historic stone daggers. The blade of the bronze dagger was less than 12 inches (30 centimeters) in length and was riveted to a wooden or bone handle.

Archaeologists have uncovered numerous daggers in the royal tombs of ancient Sumer, a civilization that arose in modern Iraq in about 4000 B.C. Many Sumerian weapons were made of solid gold, with hilts of ivory or rare stone and finely crafted sheaths (protective cases) of gold.

Eventually, smiths began to forge daggers with the blade and hilt together in one piece. At the same time, the development of iron working

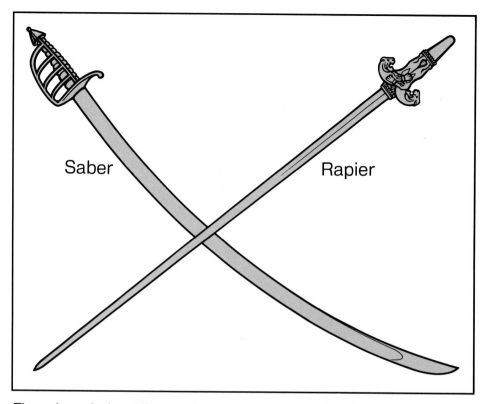

The rapier and saber differed in size and in the shape of the blade and cutting edge.

offered smiths a material hard enough and strong enough to be fashioned into the long, thin sword blade.

The Rapier and the Saber

Unlike the dagger, which was used only for stabbing, ancient warriors used the long-bladed sword for both stabbing and striking. These two methods of attack led to the development of two different types of swords.

The rapier sword was long, thin, and light with a sharp point for piercing. The heavy part of the weapon was placed near the hilt, so that the soldier could hold the tip of the weapon high and maneuver it quickly during a sword fight.

Another type of sword, the saber, was designed for slashing. The saber had a thick, heavy blade with a sharp cutting edge and was heaviest near the blade's tip. This design added extra force to the blow.

At different periods, these two types of swords rose and fell in popularity. An army that used heavy battle axes as striking weapons tended to favor the lighter rapier sword for stabbing. Armies that used spears for stabbing often preferred a sword with greater striking power like the saber.

Dual-Purpose Swords

The dual-purpose sword—one of the most important swords of ancient times—was first produced in eastern Europe. This straight, two-edged sword was heavy enough to be used for slashing but also long and pointed enough to be used as a thrusting weapon. The dual-purpose sword was quickly popularized by Greek traders who brought it to many other parts of the ancient world.

The **gladius**—a type of dual-purpose sword—was eventually adopted by the powerful Roman legion (army). The gladius was about 24 inches (60 cm) long, with a straight, two-edged blade that tapered to a sharp point.

Although light in weight, the gladius was perfectly balanced and therefore deadly when used as a saber. With a single downward stroke, a Roman soldier could split open an enemy's armor. The light weight and straight, pointed shape of the gladius also made it an effective thrusting weapon.

Soldiers of the Roman legion (army) carried the gladius—a thrusting and slashing sword—as one of their principal weapons.

The Curved Saber

The curved saber was possibly the most deadly close-range weapon of ancient times. Its ancestor was a weapon called the sickle-sword, which enjoyed great popularity in the Middle East from 2000 B.C. to

Often sheathed in an ornate case, the gladius itself had a simple design.

Gladiators fight one-on-one battles to the cheers of Roman spectators.

TO THE DEATH

In the ancient city of Rome, people gathered in large stadiums to watch pairs of specially trained warriors fight bloody, hand-to-hand battles. Viewing this competition was meant to harden the spectators toward bloodshed so that they could better endure war. The contests were also forms of entertainment and sport.

The warriors—called gladiators—were usually slaves, criminals, or prisoners of war. Successful gladiators were admired throughout Rome. To gain fame, some citizens—including military commanders and even emperors—participated in the battles. Occasionally, women also fought.

Gladiators used many different types of weapons. Some warriors fought with the deadly gladius sword and carried a large rectangular shield for protection. Others held a small, round shield and short curved sword. Some gladiators used a huge net to entangle the opponent before striking with a three-pronged spear called a trident.

Gladiators usually fought to the death, but sometimes the loser's fate depended on the audience. If the spectators turned their thumbs down, the warrior was killed. If the crowd waved their handkerchiefs, however, the loser's life could be spared.

An Egyptian pharaoh threatens a trembling enemy soldier with a short-handled sickle-sword.

1000 B.C. The sickle-sword had a curved blade set on a long, wooden handle. Sharpened on the outside of the curve, the blade curled back from the end of the shaft. The sickle-sword was a striking weapon, wielded with a whiplike swinging motion.

At first, the handle of the sickle-sword was twice as long as the blade. Over time, smiths began crafting a longer and heavier blade with a shorter handle. The sickle-sword then evolved into the curved saber that warriors used with deadly effectiveness.

EARLY MEDIUM-RANGE WEAPONS

Ancient warriors did not always engage in hand-to-hand combat. With medium-range weapons, like spears and javelins, armies could defeat their enemies from a short distance.

The Spear

Spears and javelins were quite similar in appearance—both were long, wooden shafts securely attached to sharp, metal points or blades. Both weapons were used for combat at short- and medium-range distances.

Spears were held in the hand and used for both throwing and direct stabbing. Javelins were a special type of spear, designed for throwing. Sometimes archaeologists are not entirely sure whether a particular metal point originally belonged to a spear or to a javelin.

Archaeologists do know that the spear and the javelin were constructed differently. The spear was heavy, with its weight concentrated near the tip of the blade so that the stab would be effective. Javelins were lighter and weighted toward the middle for better balance and throwing accuracy.

A Mayan warrior
stabs an enemy with
a spear. Wall murals
show that the Maya
often decorated their
spears and other
weapons before going
into battle.

The origins of these long, pointed shafts can be traced back to the simple pointed stick of prehistoric times. The earliest people took a shaft of wood, sharpened it to a point, and hardened the point with fire. They used the sticks to hunt and to dig up roots. The Greeks continued to carry these sharpened sticks into battle even after metal weapons became common.

In many ancient armies, the spear was regarded as the soldier's principal weapon. Even when metalsmiths began to make the first bronze daggers and iron swords, the spear continued to be an important weapon.

Spears had certain advantages over swords. Spears were cheaper and easier to produce, for example. Spearheads required far less metal

A painting on a Greek vase depicts ancient soldiers battling mythological Amazons (female warriors) with spears.

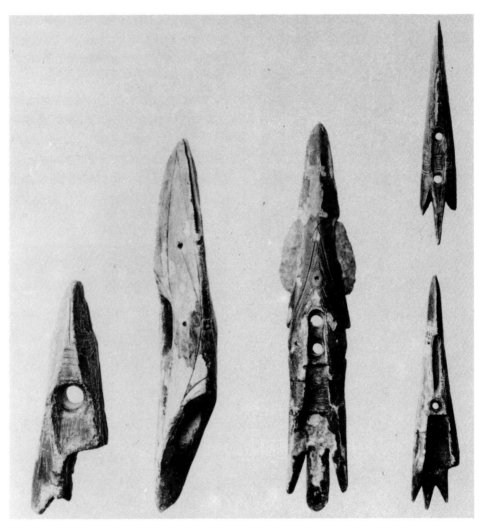

Ancient Eskimos from North America made these decorated points for harpoons—spears used mainly for hunting whales and large fish.

than swords and were smaller and simpler in design. Yet the spear's heavy wooden shaft gave it tremendous striking power. In fact, a well-made spear could pierce through almost any type of shield or armor.

The spears of ancient times, which were as much as 15 feet (4.5 meters) long, could also be used to attack opponents from a distance. Soldiers often used daggers or swords only if they failed to wound or kill the enemy with a spear.

The Phalanx

The ancient Greeks improved and expanded the use of the spear in warfare by inventing the **phalanx** —a formation of spear carriers. Soldiers lined up in a solid row with

Ancient warriors of New Caledonia—an island in the southwest Pacific Ocean— throw javelins at enemies approaching by sea.

The Javelin

Although javelins were not as common as spears, they played a key role during battle. For example, javelins could penetrate armor in situations where arrows would simply bounce off the metal harmlessly. In addition, the weight and balance of javelins allowed them to be thrown for longer distances than spears and battle axes. Between the spear and the arrow, therefore, the javelin played an important role as a medium-range weapon.

Javelin throwers were specially trained. Each warrior carried several javelins. Perhaps the best-known javelin of ancient times belonged to ordinary Roman soldiers, who were equipped with a gladius, a shield, and a javelin. This last weapon was the only one that could be used to strike an opponent from far away.

The Roman javelin had a narrow blade, a long socket, and a wooden shaft of medium length. The blade and socket were both about 30 inches (75 cm) long, and the shaft was about 5 feet (1.5 m) in length. Attached to the blade's tip was a much smaller blade that was held on by an iron bar. When the javelin struck its victim, the iron bar bent, causing the small blade to twist sideways in the wound. The twisted blade made the javelin almost impossible to pull out, and the victim usually bled to death.

The U.S. athlete Babe Didrikson prepared to throw the javelin during the 1932 Olympic Games. Many Olympic events are based on the battle skills of ancient Greek warriors.

LET THE GAMES BEGIN

The ancient Greeks believed that athletic competition honored their gods. For this reason, Greek religious festivals included contests that displayed the strength and skill of athletes.

The most important festival was the Olympic Games. This celebration was held on the sacred site of Mount Olympus to honor Zeus, the king of the gods. During this festival, warring armies stopped fighting to participate in the games.

Many Greek Olympic athletes were also warriors who used their skills in battle-related contests, such as javelin throwing and wrestling. One ancient race required foot soldiers to run in full armor while carrying a sword.

Many of the ancient Greek competitions reappeared in the modern Olympics. Athletes still throw the javelin, shoot arrows, fight with swords, and run races.

In Central America, the Maya also gathered in broad, open-air courts to watch athletes and warriors compete. One game challenged opposing teams to keep a solid rubber ball in motion without using their hands or feet. Sometimes the ball was thrown through rings attached to the sides of the courts.

The Mayan ball courts were often surrounded by temples, which symbolized the religious significance of the games. Although the games were played mainly as a form of celebration and entertainment, sometimes the losing team was killed to honor the gods.

WEAPONS FROM A DISTANCE

Long-range weapons gave a great advantage to ancient armies. The weapons allowed soldiers to move away from the enemy and still inflict great damage.

The main advantage of long-range weapons was not in their force but in the distance they could travel. An example of this is the biblical story of David, a shepherd boy, and Goliath, a mighty warrior. Goliath wore a brass helmet, a coat of mail (body protection made of many small metal links), and brass greaves (shin guards). He was armed with many weapons, including a spear and a shield.

David held only a sling, which he used to hurl stones. Struck in the head with one of these stones, Goliath was knocked unconscious before he could attack with his medium- and close-range weapons.

The Sling

The cord sling helped ancient farmers and shepherds protect their homes from attack by invaders and their flocks from attack by wild animals. The long, heavy shepherd's staff and the cord sling were an effective combination of short- and long-range weapons. Used with skill, these weapons could challenge any intruder.

A modern slingshot consists of two heavy rubber bands and a Y-shaped stick. One end of each of the bands is attached to one of the prongs of the stick. The bands are connected at the other end to a small leather pouch. The pouch holds a stone or some other ammunition. The cord sling of ancient times was much simpler. It consisted of two strings tied to a strip of leather or hide.

To operate a cord sling, the slinger placed a stone in the pouch and whirled it in the air. The faster the sling whirled, the greater the speed and force the stone would have when it was finally released. To throw the stone, the slinger let go of one of the strings, causing the pouch to open and the stone to fly

David—from the biblical story of David and Goliath—whirls a cord sling above his head. Ancient shepherds used the sling to prevent attacks on their sheep by wild animals.

out. The use of this powerful weapon required great skill.

Since leather decays rapidly, and because sling stones look just like any other round stones, it is not surprising that no ancient slings have been found. Archaeologists, however, have uncovered many paintings of soldiers using the cord sling in battle. From these records, scholars discovered that the sling was especially useful when an army attacked a fortified city. With the sling, warriors could shoot stones high enough to sail over a city's defensive walls and land inside.

The ancient Greeks eventually made sling stones out of lead instead of relying on pebbles picked up from the ground. The greater mass of the lead stone made it more wind resistant. Therefore, when thrown with the same force, the heavier lead stones traveled much farther than the light pebbles.

The Bow and Arrow

Although the sling was used effectively by ancient armies, it was never considered a basic and neces-

Armed with bows and arrows, Arabian warriors mounted on a camel attack soldiers from Assyria.

Ancient armies used bows of many different heights. This stone carving shows the Egyptian pharaoh Ramses II using a tall bow to attack his enemy from a chariot (horse-drawn battle vehicle).

sary shooting weapon. The bow and arrow, on the other hand, was the primary long-range weapon of ancient armies from the time it was first used in about 16,000 B.C. until the invention of firearms a few hundred years ago. Because the bow and arrow was such a decisive weapon in ancient conflicts, it often played a key role in the outcome of an entire war.

Throughout ancient history, people were constantly seeking ways to improve the effectiveness of the bow and arrow, mainly by trying to increase its range. Arrows were made in many shapes and sizes and served a variety of purposes. A heavy arrow could penetrate armor. A light arrow had great range but did not strike with much force.

The tip of the arrow—called the arrowhead—was made of a hard material and crafted into a sharp point. During prehistoric times, arrowheads were made of carefully

The early Indians of North America made sharp arrow points from stone.

chipped stone or bone. Eventually, weapon makers used copper, then bronze, and finally iron to form arrowheads.

Most arrowheads were either three sided or leaf shaped and had tangs for hafting. Some ancient archers, however, used long, thin, four-sided arrowheads that were shaped like pyramids. These were joined to the shafts of arrows with small sockets.

One of the most difficult tasks involved in making arrows was producing a shaft that was perfectly straight. Even a slight bend or twist in the shaft would prevent the arrow from flying straight.

To improve accuracy, feathers were attached to the end opposite the arrowhead. When set at a slight angle, feathers made the arrow spin in flight, which helped the arrow to take a straight path. The Persians (from modern Iran), who were among the best archers of ancient times, called these feathers "messengers of death."

Most arrows were about half the length of the bow, which was made in many different heights. The bow of prehistoric times was a single piece of solid wood carved into a slight curve. This simple bow, had just two parts—a wooden bow and a bowstring.

Because a piece of wood will not bend far before it breaks, the simple bow was very long, enabling a hunter or warrior to pull the bowstring back without forcing the wooden bow into a sharp curve. Some ancient archers carried simple bows that were nearly as tall as the archers themselves.

By about 3000 B.C., archers in Egypt and Mesopotamia (modern Iraq) began to develop more complex bows, including the **reinforced bow** and the **composite bow.** The reinforced bow is made with strips of wood or sinew (animal tissue). Bow makers used glue made from animal bones to attach the strips to the outward curve of the bow. These reinforcements enabled archers to bend the bows much farther.

The reinforced bow was especially important in regions where wood was scarce. For example, the ancient Eskimos, who lived in northern Asia and North America, had few trees in their natural environment. These people carved bows out of bone and then tied and reinforced them with sinew.

The American Indians used bows and arrows for war, as well as for hunting buffalo and other large animals.

This sixteenth-century illustration shows Boudicca, armed with a sword and a spear, leading her army against the Romans. A heroic figure in Celtic history, Boudicca was known as a strong leader and a great warrior.

BOUDICCA, THE WARRIOR QUEEN

During the first century A.D., the Romans were attempting to increase their power on the island of Great Britain, which was inhabited by Celtic clans. When Prasutagus, the king of the Celts, died, his territory was seized. The Romans also tortured his wife, Queen Boudicca, and enslaved Celtic nobles.

In A.D. 60, Boudicca gathered a huge army to battle the Romans. Under her leadership, Celtic warriors destroyed several Roman settlements, killing more than 70,000 Romans. Eventually, the Roman governor of Britain organized troops to stop Boudicca's army. At first, the Celts continued to push back the invaders. But within months the Celtic army was in retreat. To avoid capture by her enemies, Boudicca took a deadly poison.

Boudicca's fame as a soldier made her part of Celtic mythology. She is portrayed as a powerful warrior and protector who rides a chariot with knives attached to the wheels. The Roman historian Tacitus wrote about her successes, elaborate statues have been erected in her honor, and poets still write about her famous battle against the Roman army.

This Greek plate displays an archer carrying a composite bow, one of the most effective long-range weapons of ancient times.

The most advanced type of bow in ancient times was the composite bow. This weapon first appeared about 2500 B.C. in Mesopotamia and was soon adopted by other ancient armies. Early warriors considered the composite bow one of their most effective weapons.

The composite bow was made of several different materials—usually wood, sinew, and leather. This wide variety of materials made the bow strong and flexible. It could be bent into a deep curve and not lose its strength. Using this bow, archers could release the arrow in a smooth, even burst of power. The strongest of these bows could shoot a light arrow more than one-third of a mile (550 m).

THE POWER
OF PROTECTION

Since the development of the first weapons, people have invented ways of protecting themselves from their enemies. As weapons grew more dangerous, armor and shields were made thicker and stronger to withstand the deadly force used on the battlefield.

Ideally, warriors would have covered themselves in armor from head to toe and would have carried a shield for additional defense. In reality, a warrior weighted down by heavy armor would be almost incapable of fighting. And with one hand gripping a shield, a soldier was less able to handle a weapon.

Yet warriors who wore no protection from the axes, slings, and arrows of the enemy could not last on the battlefield. For this reason, soldiers wore armor on those parts of the body that were most vulnerable to attack, such as the head and the chest. Warriors also carried small, protective shields that allowed them to move easily.

Ancient smiths made a constant effort to find just the right balance between the need for protection and the need for lightness and mobility. Whenever a new weapon was developed, the need for defensive equipment changed. For example, when the mace appeared, armies developed the helmet to protect the head from sharp blows. Helmets made the mace ineffective, and, as a result, the weapon gradually lost importance.

The Shield

Warriors used their shields to place obstacles between themselves and the enemy. Shields could be used to protect almost any part of the body. One of the main disadvantages of the shield was that it occupied one of the warrior's hands at all times. To help their soldiers, armies often assigned each one a shield bearer, who kept the warriors protected during battle.

Weapon makers used a variety of materials to fashion shields. Although many were made of metal, the best shields were crafted from leather. Metal shields often cracked or split under the blows of swords and spears, but leather shields (or metal shields covered with leather) proved very effective against the jabs of close-range weapons.

Another effective substance for shields was wood, a plentiful material in most regions. Wooden shields were often covered with leather for beauty and for added strength. Some shields were constructed with many different kinds of wood pieced together.

Metal ornaments often decorated the front of a shield to identify the warrior who carried it. Because the

A painting on an ancient Greek vase shows soldiers carrying large, curved shields.

Archaeologists unearthed this ancient clay figure in Guatemala. The artifact shows a costumed eagle warrior dressed to celebrate victory on the battlefield.

FLYING LIKE AN EAGLE

To celebrate the end of war and to thank their gods for victory, the ancient Maya gathered in huge public squares in front of their temples. Musicians beat drums as warriors danced.

Known as eagle warriors, these dancers looked like giant birds. They dressed in ceremonial armor that was covered with feathers and wore helmets shaped like open beaks. During the celebration, the eagle warriors swooped and glided to imitate the flight of eagles. The dancing was also meant to entertain captured leaders, who were later executed as part of a religious ritual.

shields used by opposing armies were often similar, these identifying marks prevented soldiers from accidentally fighting other members within their own ranks.

The larger and heavier a shield was, the better protection it provided. A large and heavy shield, however, was harder to carry and to move into position. Just as they were constantly seeking to strike the right balance between too much and too little armor, ancient smiths were also continually trying to develop a shield that was neither too light nor too heavy.

The Helmet

Since the head is probably the most vulnerable part of the human body, helmets have long been one of the most important pieces of defensive equipment. Ancient helmets were made from thin sheets of metal. Because the metal decayed easily, few ancient helmets have survived to modern times. Archaeologists have uncovered some pieces of helmets that were mangled in battle, but they are difficult to repair or reconstruct.

Some ceremonial helmets were made of a single piece of metal beaten into the desired shape. The inside of the helmet was made to fit the head of the wearer, but the outside could be formed into almost any shape.

Armor worn by Etruscan warriors was highly decorative as well as practical. Brush-topped helmets, for example, cushioned enemy blows.

53

The earliest helmets were metal caps with knobs, crests, or horns. On some helmets, cone-shaped extensions carried crescents, horns, horsehair, plumes of feathers, and even the tails of animals. A row of small holes running around the edge of these helmets was used to attach padding material that protected the wearer's head from the bare metal.

Early helmets safeguarded the top of the head but left the ears and the back of the neck unprotected. Some helmets had flaps that covered these areas, but most of the face still remained vulnerable. In about 700 B.C., the Greeks developed a new helmet that covered the top, back, and sides of the head and curved around to protect most of the face. Only the eyes and mouth were left exposed.

This Greek helmet interfered with both the hearing and the vision of the wearer, however. For

A ceremonial helmet made of gold and silver has tiny holes around the edges that were used to attach protective padding.

Greek soldiers returned to wearing a smaller, lighter, and less protective helmet.

Body Armor

Making armor that protected the body was far more difficult than making a helmet that protected the head. To provide protection against the enemy's forceful blows, armor had to be made of a hard material that was difficult to penetrate. At the same time, body armor had to be flexible so the wearer could move freely.

One of the earliest forms of body armor—a heavy leather cape—could be easily penetrated by an arrow, a sword, or a spear. Some ancient people used quilted cloth to protect the body. Although this material kept the soldiers warm in cold weather, it offered little defense against a sharp blade.

The strongest body armor, which was made of metal, had to be light, flexible, and able to repel weapons. To meet these requirements, ancient smiths developed two different types of armor. One consisted of hundreds of small, overlapping metal scales that were sewn onto a garment of leather or heavy cloth. At first, the suits of scale armor covered almost the entire body. As time passed, the coat was made shorter, until it was only a tunic reaching to the knees.

An ancient warrior wears a domed helmet equipped with metal flaps that cover his ears and neck.

the next 200 years, the Greeks experimented with the design, but they never found a way to eliminate its disadvantages. After 500 B.C.,

55

This vase painting shows a hoplite (Greek foot soldier) spearing a Persian warrior. Hoplites, who were named for their round hoplon shields, wore breast-plates and shin guards made of bronze.

Although very flexible, this armor was also very heavy. Moreover, the many hundreds of scales that were needed for each suit of armor were difficult to produce and to sew onto the garment. For this reason, it is likely that only commanders and important warriors wore this type of armor in battle.

The second type of body armor consisted of two large bronze plates shaped to fit the front and the back of the body. Smaller strips of metal were joined to the plates to cover the neck, shoulders, and hips. Although this type of armor provided good protection, it often limited a foot soldier's movements. In later times, armorers (makers of armor) experimented with slightly different shapes to produce a suit that was both comfortable and protective.

When warriors were on horseback, armor took on new importance. The mounted soldier, a member of the **cavalry,** was an exposed target and therefore required more protection. For the cavalry, the ancient armorer could make heavier armor, because most of the armor's weight was carried by the horse rather than by the warrior. This allowed soldiers to use all their strength for fighting.

For these reasons, cavalry soldiers of ancient times gradually became heavily armored. With stronger weapons and protection, the cavalry assumed a larger share of the fighting.

The ordinary foot soldier, once the backbone of most armies, became less important. The foot soldier's metal armor was replaced with leather garments that eventually were abandoned.

As the armor of mounted soldiers became more complicated and more expensive, only the wealthy could afford to join the calvary. As a result, the upper class of a society usually made up the largest portion of the cavalry.

Assyrian archers wore long coats of scale armor.

An armed Roman cavalry soldier joins the march home from battle.

57

THE FIRST ARTILLERY

Although there were no cannons, rockets, bombs, grenades, or guided missiles in ancient times, large and fearsome machines of destruction did exist. These weapons were designed for use not only against enemy troops but also against fortified cities and towns.

The Ballista and the Catapult

The **ballista** shot heavy, arrowlike objects with a mechanism similar to that of a bow and arrow. The ballista's power came from ropes that were twisted tightly and attached to wooden levers. These levers were drawn back with great force behind an object that was placed on a track between the levers. When the levers were released, they snapped forward, sending the object hurtling into the air. A sharp object thrown in this manner could easily pierce the strongest armor, even at long distances.

The **catapult** was designed to hurl huge stones. It operated like the ballista, except that the catapult had only one large lever with a pocket at the end. A heavy stone was placed in the pocket before firing. Warriors slowly tightened the lever into firing position, and, when the trigger was pulled, the lever pitched the stone high into the air.

The catapult and ballista were most effective during the siege of a fortified city. While some soldiers

58

tried to dig under or to batter a city's stone walls, others used the catapult and ballista to keep defenders off the tops of the walls. Without the catapult and ballista, attackers would not be able to reach the walls through the mass of stones, arrows, and other weapons pelted down by the city's protectors.

If the fortifications were particularly tall, the attackers placed catapults and ballistas on top of wooden towers—called siege towers—that could be assembled at the battle site. These towers gave the catapults and ballistas greater range, enabling them to fire their heavy stones deep inside the city's walls.

Roman soldiers roll a catapult toward the walls of a fortified city.

Armies used the ballista (left) to throw long, heavy arrows at high speed. Soldiers prepare to load a catapult with a large rock (below).

Soldiers pound the walls of a city with a battering ram. Ancient armies often built sheds around the ram to protect themselves from heavy stones thrown from the top of the walls.

The Battering Ram

The battering ram—a long, heavy, wooden log with a metal tip—was the most effective weapon for breaking through the fortifications of a walled city. Using this weapon, attackers pounded against a stone wall to make a hole. Warriors enlarged the hole until they could pass through it into the city.

The battering ram got its name from the Romans, who made the metal end of the shaft in the shape of a ram's head. In early versions of the battering ram, the long, heavy beam of wood was held in the attackers' hands and simply swung back and forth. Using this method, however, the attackers had little protection from defenders on top of the wall.

The operation was improved by dragging a movable shed up to the walls of the city. The soldiers could stand under the shed and swing the battering ram while remaining sheltered from attack. The heavy beam was eventually hung from the roof of the shed by ropes. In this way, the soldiers could devote all their energies to swinging the ram and did not need to waste their strength by holding it up off the ground. Suspending the ram allowed the warriors to steady it and aim each blow at exactly the same spot on the wall.

This ancient carving shows two armies battling with bows and arrows while a battering ram strikes a fortress wall.

Defenses Against the Battering Ram

Many ancient fortifications were constructed with defenses against the battering ram. The best defense was to surround the walls with hills. If these slopes were steep enough, the heavy ram could not be wheeled close to the wall.

To attack a fortress surrounded by steep hills, an opposing army had to build a long ramp. It began some distance from the fortress and went up at a gradual slope, ending in a level area next to the wall. Although building such a ramp was slow, difficult, and dangerous, it was the only way to position the battering ram near the wall.

The giant Trojan horse hid ancient Greek soldiers as they prepared to attack the city of Troy.

TRICKING THE TROJANS

In about 1200 B.C., the ancient Greeks were fighting the Trojan War. This combat pitted Greece's army against the people of the walled city of Troy (in modern Turkey). The Greeks had been attacking Troy for 10 years without success. Unable to defeat the Trojans with strength, the Greeks developed a plan to trick their enemies into opening the city gates.

The Greeks built a huge wooden horse—known as the Trojan horse—and placed it outside the walls of Troy. Some warriors hid inside the horse while the rest of the Greek army boarded ships and sailed them out of view.

Believing that the horse was sacred and would protect them, the Trojans pulled it inside their city gates and celebrated their apparent victory over the Greek invaders. That night, while the Trojans slept, the Greek warriors crept out of the horse and opened the gates for the rest of the army, which had returned to Troy from a nearby island. The Greeks then killed most of the Trojans and set Troy on fire.

Defenders could also stop attackers by setting ramps on fire. They sometimes poured buckets of boiling oil on the leather-covered roofs of the shed and then threw down a lighted torch. This method of defense was so common that the sheds of some ancient battering rams were built to hold tanks of water for fighting fires.

Although these defenses created difficulties for the attackers, they rarely did more than postpone the inevitable. In the end, the battering ram usually succeeded in breaking through the wall, allowing a strong army to defeat the city's inhabitants. The battering ram was probably the most successful of all the large ancient war weapons.

As soldiers hit a city's walls with a battering ram (center), defenders (top right) try to stop the attack by throwing down lighted torches.

An army positions a siege tower on a portable ramp near an enemy's fortified city.

A SECRET WEAPON

One of the most feared weapons in early warfare was the mysterious mixture called Greek fire. A chemical compound, Greek fire burned furiously on water and even underwater. This dangerous weapon, which was often used in naval battles, gave off great amounts of smoke and a terrible smell. Approaching armies, upon seeing the smoke, thought twice about continuing the battle.

The Greeks kept their recipe for Greek fire a secret, but scholars believe that it contained sulfer, oil, resin, pitch, and quicklime. Shot through a tube, this mixture lit quickly and could only be put out with sand or vinegar. Although Greek fire was used mainly as a naval weapon, the Greeks also dropped it on enemies from the tops of walls and used catapults to hurl jars of the lethal mixture inside city gates.

A Greek naval crew attacks an enemy ship with Greek fire, a deadly chemical weapon.

Arrows fly through the air as two ancient armies clash with spears, swords, and shields. Modern soldiers, many of whom use computerized weapon systems, seldom come face-to-face with their enemies.

In fact, it was not replaced until the development of firearms and cannons in the Middle Ages (fifth to fifteenth centuries).

Ancient Lessons

Through the study of ancient weapons, archaeologists can learn much about different civilizations, including whether they were peaceful or aggressive, how technologically advanced they were, and how they valued human life. These weapons also help archaeologists to learn about the strategies and tactics of ancient warfare.

Ancient weapons now seem fairly harmless when compared to bombs, guns, and computerized missiles. These early weapons, however, used the same basic scientific principles that led to the development of modern arms. The remains of ancient weapons remind us that, from the very beginning, humans have armed themselves for war.

PRONUNCIATION GUIDE

ballista	(buh-LIHS-tuh)
Boudicca	(BOO-dih-kuh)
fasces	(FAHS-eez)
gladius	(GLAD-ee-uhs)
javelin	(JAV-uh-luhn)
Maya	(MY-uh)
phalanx	(FAY-langks)
rapier	(RAY-pee-uhr)
saber	(SAY-buhr)
Sumer	(SOO-muhr)
Trojan	(TROH-juhn)

Sculpted in about 400 B.C., this relief portrays Athena, the Greek goddess of war. According to Greek mythology, Athena's father, Zeus—the king of the gods—entrusted her with his shield and his mightiest weapon, the thunderbolt.

GLOSSARY

archaeologist: a scientist who studies the material remains of past human life.

armor: metal or leather covering worn to protect the body against weapons.

artifact: any object made by a human. Artifacts can include items crafted from natural materials, such as bone, stone, clay, or wood.

ballista: a large ancient weapon shaped like a bow and arrow for shooting pointed objects from a distance.

catapult: a large, long-range weapon used by ancient armies to hurl huge stones. A pocket at the end of a lever held the stone. When the lever was released, the stone flew through the air.

cavalry: soldiers who fight on horseback.

composite bow and reinforced bow: types of ancient bows made from many different materials, including wood, bone, leather, and sinew (animal tissue). These materials were combined for strength and flexibility.

gladius: a double-edged sword used by ancient Roman soldiers.

haft: to attach the metal blade of a tool or weapon to a handle.

hilt: the handle of a sword or dagger.

Archaeologists uncovered this clay figure of an ancient soldier in Central Asia.

phalanx: a battle formation in which soldiers stand shoulder to shoulder. Each soldier holds a shield in one hand and a spear in the other. Both the spear and the shield are pointed outward.

rivet: a metal bolt used for fastening objects, such as the blade of a weapon to a handle.

scavenger: a person who gathers usable materials. In ancient times, scavengers collected food, building materials, and other necessities from their natural surroundings.

smith: a person who makes or repairs metal objects.

tang: a point or prong on a tool or weapon that fits into a handle.

tomahawk: a small, light ax used by American Indians as a weapon or tool.

INDEX

This hunting scene—found on a tomb in Sidon, Lebanon—depicts an army fighting animals with battle axes and shields.

70

An Assyrian relief excavated from the ancient ruins of Nimrud (in modern Iraq) shows warriors using a ladder to attack the walls of a fortified city.

Photo Acknowledgments

p. 2, Theodora Wilbour Fund in Memory of Zoë Wilbour, Courtesy, Museum of Fine Arts, Boston; p. 7, Office of the State Archaeologist, University of Iowa; pp. 8, 14, 17, 18, 19, 22, 23, 25, 26, 27 (bottom), 31 (top and bottom), 33, 37, 39, 40, 43, 44, 45, 49, 51, 52, 53, 54, 55, 56, 57 (top), 62, 64, 70, 71, Independent Picture Service; p. 9, University of Michigan Museum of Anthropology; pp. 10 (top), 28, 69, The Nelson-Atkins Museum of Art; pp. 10 (bottom), 68, Minneapolis Public Library and Information Center; p. 11, Tennessee State Museum/painting by Carlyle Urello; p. 12, Wilford Archaeology Laboratory, University of Minnesota/by Kathy Raskob/IPS; p. 13, Landesmuseum Joanneum Graz, Department of Prehistory and Early History; pp. 15, 57, 59, 63, 67, The Bettmann Archive; pp. 16, 29, Fitzwilliam Museum, University of Cambridge; p. 21, Stuart Rome; p. 24, U.S. Capitol Historical Society; pp. 27 (top), 30, Laura Westlund; pp. 32, 36, The Mansell Collection; p. 35, The Carnegie Institution of Washington, D.C., Publication 602; p. 38, Werner Forman Archive/ Statens Historiska Museum, Stockholm; p. 41, United States Olympic Committee; p. 46, Haffenreffer Museum of Anthropology, Brown University; p. 47, National Archives of Canada, Ottawa (C-114467); p. 48, The British Library; pp. 60 (top and bottom), 61, 65, Picture Collection, The Branch Libraries/ The New York Public Library; p. 66, National Library, Madrid.

Cover photographs: University of Michigan Museum of Anthropology (front) and National Archives of Canada, Ottawa (C-114467) (back).